THE Toothpaste
SECRET

TRISHA E. O'HEHIR

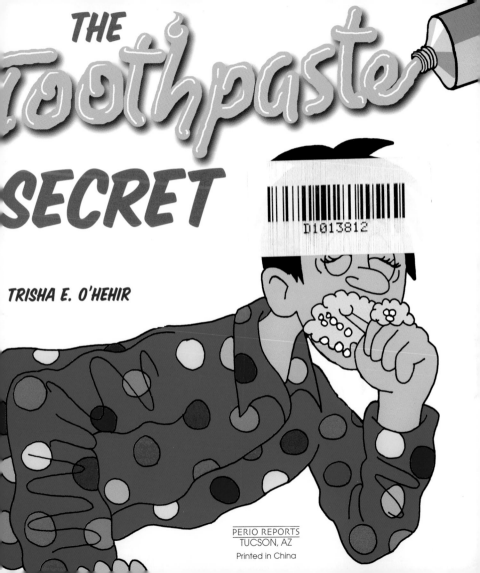

D1013812

PERIO REPORTS
TUCSON, AZ
Printed in China

Published by
Perio Reports
P.O. Box 30367
Flagstaff, AZ 86003-0367

Publisher's Cataloging-in-Publication Data
O'Hehir, Trisha E.
     The toothpaste secret / Trisha E. O'Hehir.–Tucson, AZ:
Perio Reports, 2003.

     p.   ;   cm.

     ISBN 0-9659236-1-4
     1. Teeth–Care and hygiene–Juvenile literature. I. Title.

RK63 .034 2003   2002111128
613–dc21   0301

06 05 04 03 02 • 5 4 3 2 1

Project coordination by Jenkins Group, Inc. • www.bookpublishing.com
Book design by Kelli Leader

Printed in China

Dedicated to the
memory of
John Furman,
a talented cartoonist who
became an advocate for
dry toothbrushing through
this project.

EVERYBODY

brushes with toothpaste.

TOOTHPASTE makes so many bubbles you can't see in the mirror, so you just drool and daydream. Thirty seconds seems like three minutes.

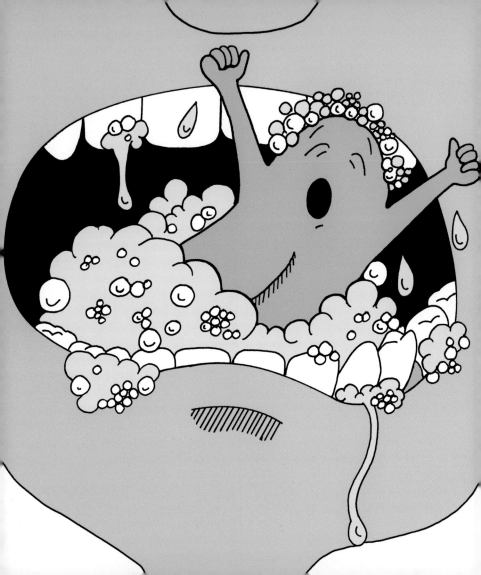

TOOTHPASTE

flavor numbs your tongue so your teeth feel clean when they really aren't.

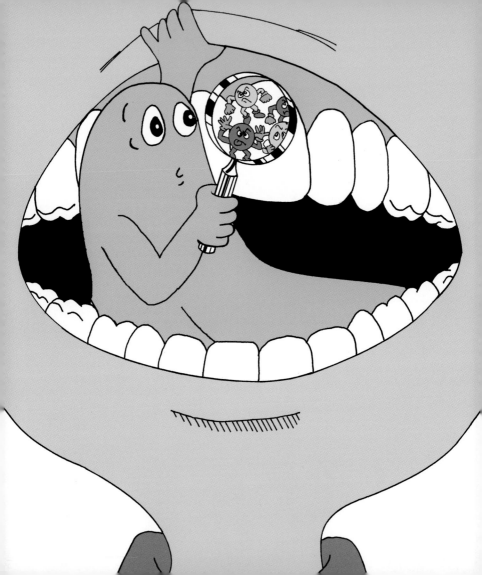

HOW CAN

you tell where the bacteria
are in your mouth?

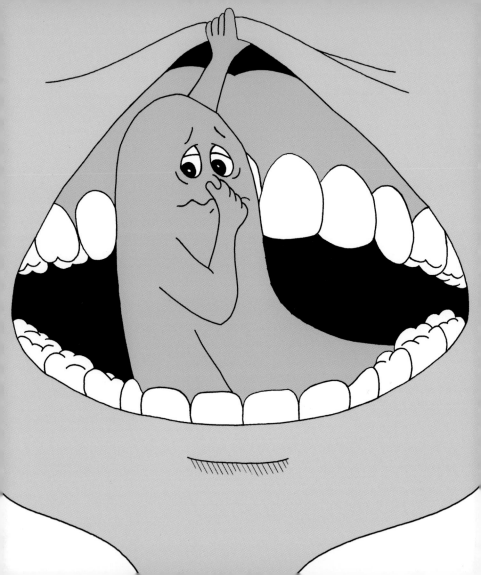

YOU CAN'T SEE
the bacteria, but you
can smell them when
you wake up in the morning.
MORNING MOUTH!

Some say it
smells like the bottom of a
GYM LOCKER.

You can also feel the
BACTERIAL PLAQUE
with your tongue.

Some people say
it feels like the teeth are
wearing SWEATERS.

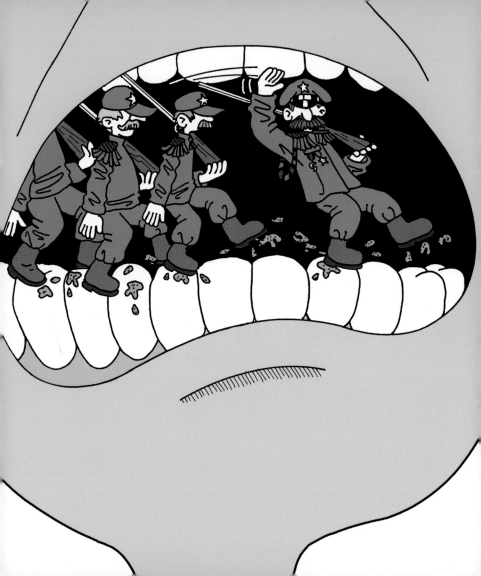

Some say it feels like the
ARMY MARCHING
THROUGH.

Some say it feels
like the bottom of a
BIRD CAGE.

Some say it feels like
paw prints at the ZOO.

And some say
it just feels FUZZY!

Too bad plaque isn't GREEN, then we could see it!

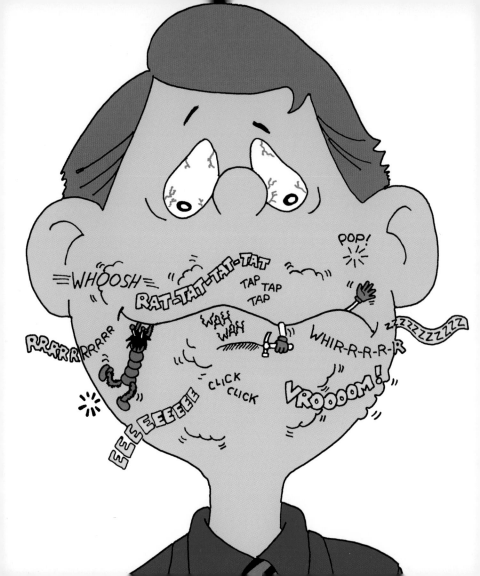

MILLIONS
of bacteria are making
a home in your mouth
right now.

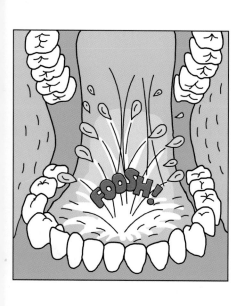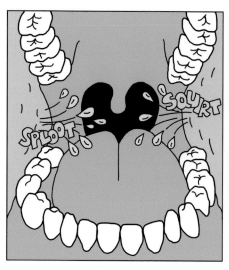

JUST ADD SALIVA

and the plaque will harden.
Saliva ducts are in your
cheeks and under
your tongue.

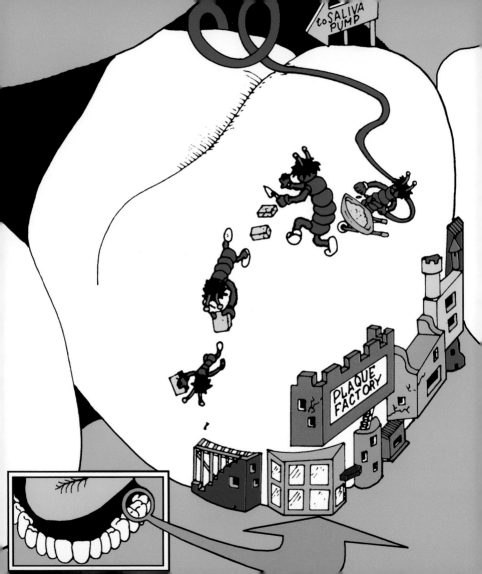

IN JUST ONE DAY,

soft plaque hardens
into tartar.

BACTERIA USE THE

minerals in the saliva to form a cement-like material.

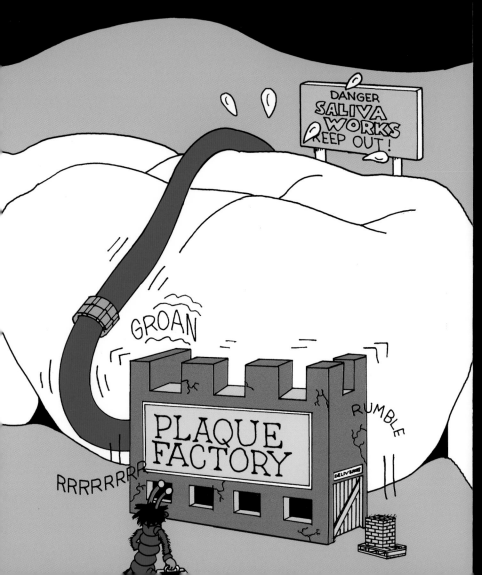

...ALMOST LIKE BRICKS.

The BACTERIA build houses, apartments, and shopping centers on the back of your front teeth.

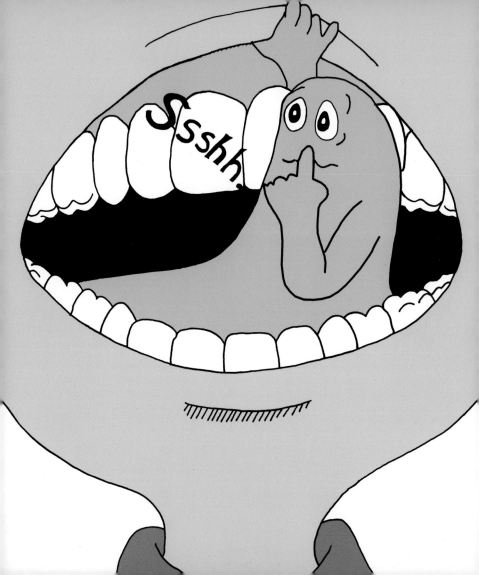

If you know the

TOOTHPASTE SECRET,

you can remove sticky bacteria, prevent tartar buildup and have fresh breath.

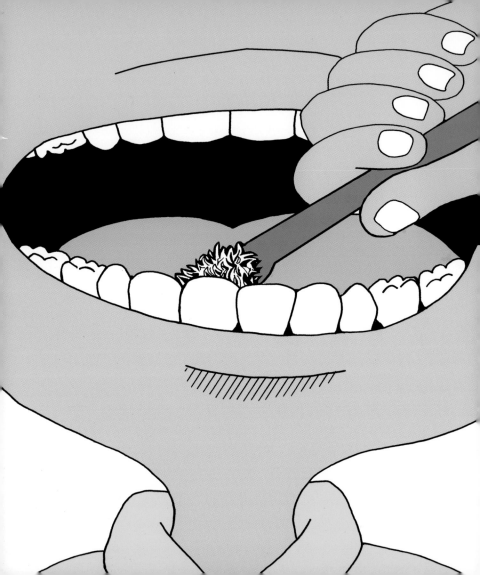

All you have to do is DRY BRUSH.

Start on the INSIDE OF THE BOTTOM TEETH and brush until all your teeth feel clean and taste clean— then add toothpaste.

Here's the 2-part
brushing method.

PART 1

Brush dry until your
teeth feel clean.
Remember – no water
and no toothpaste.

PART 2

Now add toothpaste
to polish and put fluoride
on your teeth.

Your teeth will be so clean
your dental hygienist will ask

"WHAT HAVE YOU
BEEN DOING?"

Just smile and say
"IT'S A SECRET!"

THE *TOOTHPASTE* SECRET

This book is the first in the
"Dental Secret Series"

Other titles coming soon:

THE DENTAL FLOSS SECRET

THE GUM DISEASE SECRET

THE TOOTH DECAY SECRET

Reserve your copy now for only
$9.95 plus $2.00 S & H for each book.
Order 50 copies or more and get a 20% discount.

Dental Secrets
P.O. Box 30367
Flagstaff, AZ 86003-0367

To order:
www.ToothpasteSecret.com
1-800-374-4290
Fax: 520-323-5602

Name_____

Address _____

City _____ State _____ Zip_____

Telephone_____ e-mail _____

The Toothpaste Secret _____ copies

Visa/MasterCard_____

Exp Date _____ / _____

Printed in China